contents

introduction

If you think you can or think you can't, you're usually right.
Henry Ford

It has taken me most of my life to realise the truth behind success, which is this: success is not a matter of luck, it is a matter of design.

I believe that success is a personal experience and best defined as the gradual realisation of your goals, both personal and professional. Wealth, happiness and the rest are simply by-products created by the achievement of these goals. Winners don't *get* more opportunities – they *create* them. They don't let setbacks reinforce a poor self-image; they see them as opportunities in disguise, as chances to bolster their resolve to succeed in realising their dreams.

Whatever dream you have for your future, provided it is realistic, it is within the realms of the achievable.

This book will no more make you successful than joining a gym will make you fit, because the critical ingredient is you; your commitment, determination and application. No one can do it for you. It is my deepest wish that I may help you believe this: you can. Because I know that when you believe you can, you will.

the wake-up call

At the age of twenty-nine, and poised for the first time to achieve a real degree of success, Robin was diagnosed with cancer. Like so many of us, Robin felt that his destiny was ultimately in somebody else's hands. So rather than going out to make the success he wanted happen, he was waiting for it to happen to him. The diagnosis of cancer was his wake-up call.

Over the next few years he read, studied and talked to those whose experiences he could learn from, distilling the recurring principles into a clear, simple and effective form. Understanding that knowledge alone is not power, Robin developed ways of living his life in a more focused, positive manner leading to a transformation which was as dramatic as it was immediate and tangible.

The components of success are universal, timeless and constant. Successful people and businesses are winners on the inside. Success is an internal feeling with external manifestations.
Robin Sieger

Robin has taken a wealth of experience and distilled it into 'Natural Born Winners'. Whoever you are, whatever your circumstances, the 'Natural Born Winners' programme can help be your passport to success.

Some people make things happen, some watch things happen, and some wonder what happened.
Anon

Luck is what happens when preparation meets opportunity.
Seneca the Elder

Opportunity is missed by most people because it is dressed in overalls and looks like work.
Thomas Edison

If your train's on the wrong track, every station you come to is the wrong station.
Bernard Malamud

Two men look through prison bars: one sees mud, the other stars.
Frederick Langbridge

Do the thing you fear, and the death of fear is certain.
Ralph Waldo Emerson

success

The quality of our self-image – positive or negative – is central to our potential for success. The you you see is the you you'll be. If you have a poor self-image, you will always be looking for evidence to reflect or confirm this belief. Start to see and think of yourself as a success, right now. To achieve success, however, we need to recognise that failure is part of the learning process. When we fail, it just means that we are not doing it – whatever it may be – right.

Your beliefs at a corporate and, more importantly at a personal level, represent your core values. Our true beliefs must be about believing that the goal we have set out to realise already exists in the future. If you believe with one hundred per cent certainty that success is achievable, and that failures along the way are no more than life offering you learning experiences, you will create a strong inner confidence that needs no image consulting or window dressing.

The 'you' that people meet will be an individual with a very clear idea of where 'you' are going. Your core beliefs will permeate your thinking and the way you think will impact directly on how you perform, how the world perceives you and will give substance to your life.

Our self-image and our habits tend to go together. Change one, and you automatically change the other.
Maxwell Maltz

Death is not the greatest loss in life. The greatest loss in life is what dies inside us while we live.
Norman Cousins

There is never a wrong time to do the right thing.
Anon

Save worry and anxiety for the major upsets in life. Today make a conscious effort to see something positive in every situation.
Anon

Good people are good because they've come to wisdom through failure. We get very little wisdom from success, you know.
William Saroyan

Each problem that I solved became a rule which served afterwards to solve other problems.
Rene Descartes

from
today

think of yourself as

successful

and remember

action follows thought

you the hero

I believe that within every person there is a hero with whom we have lost contact. That hero has an absolute conviction in his/her ability to succeed. The success we're talking about is not winning awards or medals for acts of courage in battlefields. It's about being able to stand up every time you fall, believing that no matter how often you fall, you have the determination to get up one more time.

Ninety-six per cent of four-year-olds have high self-esteem. They believe that they can do anything they want to. But by the time they are eighteen, fewer than five per cent have retained this belief. It is very important that we reconnect with those positive self-images from our childhood, because when we do, we reinforce them at a subconscious level. And every time we achieve something that we would naturally shy away from, we are forming a powerful positive memory, building a stronger self-belief and further expanding the limits of our horizon.

A winner is simply someone who got up one more time than they fell down.

To be a winner, whatever your endeavour, it is you and you alone who must persist in making the effort to realise your goal. Whatever your life circumstances, your starting point is not an indicator of where you are capable of going. I believe that the real tragedy in life is not failing to reach our goals, but not having goals to aspire to.

Being a champion means thinking like a champion – visualise the rewards of your success, and stay positive. So commit yourself to the journey and take that first step. A dream that generates action will change your world, so don't be afraid to dream big!

Just think how happy you would be if you lost everything you have right now, and then got it back again.
Anon

When schemes are laid in advance, it is surprising how often circumstances fit in with them.
Sir William Osler

Give me a stock clerk with a goal and I'll give you a man who will make history. Give me a man with no goals and I'll give you a stock clerk.
J C Penney

Make the most of every failure. Fall forward.
Anon

Press on. Nothing can take the place of persistence. Talent will not; the world is full of unsuccessful people with talent. Genius will not; unrewarded genius is almost a proverb. Education alone will not; the world is full of educated derelicts. Persistence and determination alone are omnipotent.
Calvin Coolidge

Within you right now is the power to do things you never dreamed possible. This power becomes available to you just as soon as you can change your beliefs.
Maxwell Maltz

from
today

believe you can

and you will

and remember

you only truly fail
when you quit,

so don't give up

the big secret

No doubt many of us would love to discover a magic recipe for success. A formula that would bestow wealth, joy and happiness on its finder. However, after many years of searching for this magic recipe, I can finally reveal the big secret to being a winner: *there is no secret.* The reality is winners come in all shapes and sizes but all have this in common: they have achieved their own personal goal by following four natural principles for success:

A clear goal
A definite plan
Confidence
No fear of failure

And here is the best news of all. Evolution instilled these qualities in each and every one of us at birth. Although most of us have allowed these qualities to atrophy, forgetting we ever had them, the good news is that they can be relearned.

When we see a successful person we tend only to see their success, never their journey. But look a little closer and you will see evidence of the four principles. The reality is that the basic ingredients of achievement are neither complex nor obscure. You were born with them. You just need to start believing in them and then the magic begins.

This is your life - it is your journey. Don't let fear of failure stop you from trying to reach your goal for there is no shame in failing, the only shame is in never trying.

Godlike Genius? Godlike nothing - sticking to it is the genius.
Thomas Edison

Your life is up to you, life provides the canvas, you do the painting.
Anon

My own experience has taught me this: if you wait for the perfect moment when all is safe and assured it may never arrive. Mountains will not be climbed, races won or lasting happiness achieved.
Maurice Chevalier

Your life is what your thoughts make it.
Marcus Aurelius

It is not enough to have a good mind; the main thing is to use it well.
Rene Descartes

Watch your thoughts; they become words.
Watch your words; they become actions.
Watch your actions; they become habits.
Watch your habits; they become character.
Watch your character; it becomes your destiny.
Frank Outlaw

from today

confidently take

the next step

and remember

you can do it

attitude

The one thing in the world you have 100% control over, is your attitude. Pure and simple. Sometimes we choose to have a poor attitude because it allows us to justify our failures, our setbacks, and also stops us from taking responsibility for our lives.

This ability to consciously choose our attitude is an essential ingredient in creating success and a feature of high performing individuals. If you begin to focus with a positive attitude, you will begin to put setbacks in perspective and not dwell on failure. You will begin to act in accordance with a healthy and positive self-image. Learn to develop and program a positive, success-orientated attitude that operates subconsciously twenty-four hours a day. The means of doing this are simple. Think of it as changing computer software; exchange negative habits and thinking patterns which have created mechanisms that subconsciously cause you to fail, with positive affirming thought patterns and habits.

The attitude you should develop is a humble yet strong inner belief. Not some unrealistic delusional behaviour that ignores reality, but a quiet heartfelt optimism in your ability to let nothing steal your dream or divert you from your goal.

Attitude is the difference that makes the difference. In the course of our lives we will all experience failure and upset. Some minor experiences can be life changing and others catastrophic. Our ability to succeed is not measured by what happens to us in life, but by what we choose to do about it. Your attitude determines your ability to respond positively.

The tragedy in life is not in failing to realise one's goals, but in failing to have goals to realise.
Isaiah Mayes

One never goes as far when one doesn't know where one is going.
Goethe

What you think of yourself is much more important than what others think of you.
Seneca the Elder

We make a living by what we get, we make a life by what we give.
Sir Winston Churchill

Formulate and indelibly stamp on your mind a mental picture of yourself as succeeding. Hold this picture tenaciously. Never permit it to fade – and your mind will seek to develop the picture.
Norman Vincent Peale

I am one, but I am only one. I cannot do everything; but I will not let what I cannot do interfere with what I can do.
Edward Everett Hale

from today

live in the now

with a fully functioning
positive attitude

and remember

your attitude is
your choice

clear goals

In all aspects of your life, as in all aspects of your business, you deserve better than O.K. What you should be aiming for is great, fantastic, and wonderful! Remember, the ability to consistently define goals in clear and succinct terms is a common feature of successful individuals.

Set your goals not only in your mind, but also in your heart. For true success, you need to feel a desire to reach your goal that is so great that it occupies both your head and your heart. If we understand that success at a personal level is the gradual realisation of our individual goals, then small incremental steps towards our goals are successes too, and each step we take that brings us closer to our long term goals is a step successfully taken.

Starting any journey or endeavour requires us to act confidently and promptly without hesitation. Your chance is now. Every day can be a fresh start. Write down all the reasons why you should start now. This in itself will strengthen your resolve. As your self-esteem increases from your small successes, so the journey will become more meaningful and you will become more enthusiastic, more confident – and happier.

There is a giant asleep within every man.
When the giant awakes, miracles happen.
Frederick Faust

There is only the moment. The now. Only what you are
experiencing at this second is real. This does not mean you live
for the moment. It means you live in the moment.
Leo Buscaglia

Rules for being human;
You will learn lessons. There are no mistakes – only lessons.
A lesson is repeated until it is learned.
If you don't learn lessons, they get harder (pain is one way the
universe gets your attention). You'll know you've learned a
lesson when your actions change.
Anon

Go out on a limb – that's where the fruit is.
Will Rogers

Never mistake a single defeat for a final defeat.
F Scott Fitzgerald

from today

clearly define

    your goals
    write them down

and remember

    revisit them every day

plan, plan, plan

In the absence of a plan we have random chance, pure and simple! Planning is as natural to the process of success as its absence is to the process of failure. Have a plan and keep it simple. Remember, a chain is only as strong as its weakest link.

There are two simple questions you need to answer:

1 Where do I want to go?
2 When do I want to get there?

Create a blueprint for your goal and *write it down*. The written plan is a guide to which you can return daily, examine your progress and, if necessary, adapt or change. This might sound too simple - but it works and lets you know if you're on target. Think about it this way. When you go on vacation the first thing you plan is the destination (clearly defined goal), then you plan your route. Due to circumstances beyond your control you may have to change your route, but the destination will remain the same.

Change is the one thing that we encounter continually. If your plan is rigid, if it cannot bend, it will break down and you may lose momentum, so keep your plan flexible. If the time frame for achieving your goal proves too short, then extend it, reset the date. If you allow yourself the flexibility to change your blueprint as you go along, you won't be demoralised by changes when they occur.

Study the strategies used by those who have accomplished what you are seeking to achieve. Learn from their experiences and be inspired by them.

A belief is not merely an idea that the mind possesses, it is an idea that possesses the mind.
Robert Bolton

According to the theory of aerodynamics, the bumblebee is unable to fly. This is because the size, weight and shape of its body in relation to the total wing spread make flying impossible. But the bumblebee, being ignorant of these profound scientific truths, goes ahead and flies anyway and also manages to make a little honey every day.
Anon

Come to the edge, He said. They said: we are afraid. Come to the edge, He said. They came. He pushed them and they flew.
Guillaume Apollinaire

Self-doubt is nature's way of giving us a reality check.
We can easily forgive a child who is afraid of the dark; the real tragedy of life is when adults are afraid of the light.
Plato

No one can make you feel inferior without your consent.
Eleanor Roosevelt

from
today

leave nothing to chance

work out what you
need to do, then do it

and remember

change it as often as
you need to,
then do that instead!

confidence

Confidence is the ability to believe in something without necessarily having any firm evidence for it. The ability to believe in yourself is the foundation of your confidence, and positive experiences serve to reinforce it. Self-doubt is natural, even for people at the top of their profession, but the important thing is to put self-doubt in perspective. Understand that everyone has these moments, they're normal, just don't fear them or let them immobilise you.

Faith is simply a belief for which there is no absolute proof. If you create a positive self-belief, with faith in yourself and your ability to succeed, you are maximising your potential to create success.

We are born without any sense of externally imposed limits on our potential. We enter this world as natural born winners, so put yourself in touch with the child you were; feel again the sense of wonderment and the belief that anything is possible. Draw on those childlike qualities of imagination and determination and if you do something well, something that pleases you, give yourself a quiet, "Well done!" Develop your confidence by keeping a positive self-image, and celebrate every success no matter how small.

The truth that many people never understand until it is too late, is that the more you try to avoid suffering the more you suffer, because small and more insignificant things begin to torture you in proportion to your fear of being hurt.
Thomas Merton

Those who try to do something and fail are infinitely better than those who try to do nothing and succeed.
Richard Bird

Never give in – never, never, never give in.
Winston Churchill

Obstacles are those frightful things you see when you take your eyes off your goal.
Henry Ford

Ideas are like rabbits. You get a couple and learn how to handle them, and pretty soon you have a dozen.
John Steinbeck

Fail fast and fail often.
Thomas Watson Snr

from today

have faith in yourself

never allow doubt to
cloud over your dream

and remember

your confidence will
grow daily

no fear of failure

Natural born winners have learned the 'So what?' attitude to failure. They truly believe that they will ultimately succeed and are committed to the process so, when problems come along, they take the view that they will overcome them. Don't mistake this for the 'Who cares?' attitude which is fundamentally alien to success and in consequence gives up. Failure is never final unless you determine it to be so, so have faith in your ability to recover from setbacks.

As a child you learned to walk by falling over. According to research a child falls over an average of 240 times in the process of learning to master the complex art of defying gravity and balancing whilst moving forward (walking to you and me). We learned to walk by having no fear of failure, by repeated encouragement from our family and through a never say die ability to persist.

Most people fear failure because of what other people may think. The truth is, nobody really cares and once you accept that failure is your first step to success, then you are truly on your way. When you close in on your goal, whatever it may be, do so with the uncluttered and fearless approach of the child within, and go for it.

Many persons have the wrong idea of what constitutes true happiness. It is not attained through self-gratification, but through fidelity to a worthy purpose.
Helen Keller

Take away my people but leave my factory and soon grass will be growing on the shop floor; however, take away my factory and leave me my people, and we will build another business.
Andrew Carnegie

We don't remember days; we remember moments.
Cesare Pavese

Joy is not in things, it is in us.
Richard Wagner

You will find, as you look back upon life, that the moments that stand out are the moments when you have done things for others.
Henry Drummond

It is one of the most beautiful compensations of life that no man can sincerely try to help another without helping himself.
Ralph Waldo Emerson

so today

learn from your failures, don't
identify with them

everyone experiences
failure, but always see
the positive and just
don't quit

and remember

each failure brings you a
step closer to success

motivation

The word 'motivation' means *motive* and *action* – when you are seeking to achieve something you *move* towards your objective. But what *is* your motive? It will be the force that will drive you on. Identify what motivates you; your internal motive will drive your determination to change. Setbacks and crises can be great motivators. Many people who experience a personal crisis (loss of job, loss of a loved one) later say it was the event that enabled them to make a radical change in outlook.

Your core values and your passion for what you are doing are the strongest motivators when it comes to how you act, think and work. What is *your* passion? Identify it and get it to work for you. Identify your core values. When our values are at odds with our goal, success will almost certainly elude us – or if it doesn't elude us, it won't last long because it will be built on shallow foundations. I am talking about personal integrity, for in the pursuit of personal and professional success, it is important that you do the 'right thing'.

Ultimately the values and true success that we seek are realised at a spiritual level, when we reach the understanding that success, joy and happiness lie not in things, places or people, but within ourselves. Nevertheless, sometimes being nice for the sake of it has its own rewards, whatever you believe!

This is the only chance you will have on earth with this exciting adventure called life. So why not plan it and try to live it as richly, as happily, as possible?
Anon

If you can dream it, you can do it.
Walt Disney

The greatest discovery of my generation is that a human being can alter his life by altering the attitude of his mind.
William James

To laugh often and much; to win the respect of intelligent people and the affection of children; to earn the appreciation of honest critics and endure the betrayal of false friends; to appreciate beauty; to find the best in others; to leave the world a bit better, whether by a healthy child, a garden patch or a redeemed social condition; to know even one life has breathed easier because you have lived. This is to have succeeded.
Ralph Waldo Emerson

so today

find your passion,
values and purpose

then you'll discover
your motivation

and remember

success is an
experience of the journey,
not the destination

new beginnings

There is a professor at a university in America who said to all of his new students on their first day; 'If I could buy you for what you think you are worth and sell you for what I *know* you are worth, I'd be a millionaire.' Think of yourself in terms of your potential, just like a business, a good investment for the future! To be truly happy and successful you need to be operating as efficiently as a well run business. So let's look at the seven aspects of your life that you need to work on to stay on track towards your goal.

Self	How do you feel about yourself? Develop a positive self image.
Health	Are you taking care of your physical and mental well-being?
Attitude	Do you have a positive attitude? – don't settle for O.K. Strive for fantastic!
Relationship	How is your relationship with yourself and others?
Spirit	Do you reflect upon what it is that you are doing with your life?
Career	Do you have a clear goal?
Wealth	Take care of the first six and this will take care of itself!

Make sure that you are operating these seven aspects at a level 'fantastic'. If you are having problems, seek help, ask a friend, read a book, join a night class, get tuition, do something to improve. Don't wait for something to happen. Make it happen!

Finally

At the end of our lives we don't regret the things at which we failed – we regret the things we wished for but never attempted.

Robin Sieger

so today

remember you are a unique
individual

the world has never seen your
like before

you make the difference

so

dream big, dare greatly,
shine brightly -

YOU CAN DO IT!

about the author

Robin Sieger is a success strategist, author and renowned motivational speaker. His company has built an international reputation as being a powerful catalyst for change. Using breakthrough initiatives, the Sieger Group helps companies, organisations and individuals alike to create a success culture where potential turns into progress.

In addition to his corporate commitments, Robin works with charities and has developed the 'No Limits'™ self-esteem programme for school children. He also runs the Natural Born Winners ™ seminar for the public during the year.

A world class keynote speaker, he is noted for his humour and ability to inspire, motivate and transform audiences internationally. His corporate training, consulting and speaking clients include: Blockbuster, British Aerospace, British Telecom, Coca Cola, HSBC, IBM, Macdonalds, Microsoft, Toshiba and Unichem.

For information on keynote presentations, seminars, consulting, training and products, please contact The Sieger Group.

Tel: 0800 917 2938
E-mail: robin@siegergroup.com
www.siegergroup.com

notes